D0792230

*T1-AYO-201*

# GENETICS EXPERT

## JOANNA L. KELLEY

LAURA HAMILTON WAXMAN

**Lerner Publications**
Minneapolis

The publisher wishes to thank Joanna L. Kelley for providing some of the photos that appear in this book.

For Yana, an inquisitive nature lover —L.H.W.

Lerner Publications Company
A division of Lerner Publishing Group, Inc.
241 First Avenue North
Minneapolis, MN 55401 USA

For reading levels and more information, look up this title at www.lernerbooks.com.

Content Consultant: David Greenstein, PhD, Professor of Genetics, Cell Biology and Development, University of Minnesota

Library of Congress Cataloging-in-Publication Data

Waxman, Laura Hamilton, author.
    Genetics expert Joanna L. Kelley / by Laura Hamilton Waxman.
        pages    cm. — (STEM trailblazer bios)
    Includes index.
    ISBN 978-1-4677-5795-9 (lib. bdg. : alk. paper) — ISBN 978-1-4677-6120-8 (pbk.) — ISBN 978-1-4677-6284-7 (EB pdf)
        1. Kelley, Joanna L.—Juvenile literature. 2. Geneticists—Biography—Juvenile literature. 3. Scientists—Biography—Juvenile literature. 4. Genomics—Juvenile literature. I. Title. II. Series: STEM trailblazer bios.
QH429.2.K45W39  2015
576.5092—dc23                                                    2014020833

Manufactured in the United States of America
1 – PC – 12/31/14

The images in this book are used with the permission of: © Lenin Arias Rodriguez, p. 4; © iStockphoto.com/Trifonov_Evgeniy, p. 5; © Comstock Images, p. 7; © Henry Moore Jr. BCU/WSU, p. 9; © age fotostock/SuperStock, p. 10; © ROBYN BECK/Getty Images, p. 11; © Alexandre Fagundes De Fagundes/Dreamstime.com, p. 13; © iStockphoto.com/STEEX, p. 14; © brookpeterson/flickr.com (CC BY-ND 2.0), p. 16; © Minden Pictures/SuperStock, p. 17; © Michael Tobler, pp. 18, 22; © WILDLIFE GmbH/Alamy, p. 19; Tasteofcrayons/Wikimedia Commons, p. 20; © Anup Shah/The Image Bank/Getty Images, p. 21; AP Photo/PR NEWSWIRE, p. 24; © Andre Jenny/Alamy, p. 25; © Enakshi Singh, p. 26; © Paul Morigi/Getty Images for Girl Scouts of America, p. 27.

Front cover: © Michael Tobler.

Main body text set in Adrianna Regular 13/22. Typeface provided by Chank.

# CONTENTS

## Chapter 1

Joanna L. Kelley has spent her life studying biology, or the science of living things.

# A CURIOUS GIRL

**J**oanna Lynne Kelley was born curious. It helped that she grew up in a family that loved math and science. Joanna's father was a mathematician. Her mother was a

**biologist**. They encouraged their kids to ask lots of questions. At dinner, they often challenged their children with math and science problems.

The Kelley parents also encouraged Joanna and her older siblings to explore nature. Joanna spent many happy hours outdoors as a kid in the 1980s. Someday, she hoped to learn more about how the natural world worked.

From an early age, Joanna was curious about the natural world.

## THE EXCITING WORLD OF GENOMICS

While young Joanna was making discoveries in her backyard, a bigger discovery was taking place. Scientists in the field of **genomics** had developed some new and exciting technology. This technology had the power to decode the entire **genome** of a plant, an animal, or another living thing. A genome is like an instruction manual for how an **organism** is created. It includes all the organism's **genes**, which are part of its **DNA**. An organism's **traits** depend on this chemical code.

In 1996, when Joanna was a teenager, a group of genome scientists made an important announcement. They had decoded the entire genome for yeast. Yeast is a small organism made of a single cell. But its genome was the largest to be fully mapped so far. The scientists had studied it to better understand the building blocks of life. They hoped to do the same for more complex organisms. Their biggest goal was to map the genome for humans.

Every organism contains DNA. DNA is made up of long twisting strands of genetic material. The shape of the strands is called a double helix.

## OFF TO COLLEGE

Kelley probably wasn't thinking much about genomics during her teen years. At the time, her main interest was math. She decided to major in math at college. In 1999, she headed to Brown University in Rhode Island. There she soaked up her professors' knowledge.

Kelley also shared knowledge of her own. She helped teach math students and professors to use difficult computer software. The software allowed people to work on complex math problems. Kelley wrote detailed instructions for the software. It was a big accomplishment. But there were many more accomplishments to come.

As Kelley continued her studies, her interests expanded. She still loved math. But she loved it because it was connected to nature. Math helped explain how life worked. Kelley's real passion was the natural world. So she decided to major in biology too. She would use both math and science to discover more about the world around her.

Kelley was a talented math and science student at Brown University.

## Chapter 2

Kelley graduated from Brown University with degrees in both math and biology.

# QUESTIONS AND ANSWERS

**W**hile Kelley found success at Brown, an international group of scientists celebrated a major success of their own. In 2003, they announced that they had decoded the genome for humans. Their work was called the Human

Genome Project. The scientists had created a complete map of human DNA, including human genes. It revealed the blueprint for what makes a human a human.

## STUDYING GENOMICS

The same year the Human Genome Project was completed, Kelley graduated from college. She had earned degrees in math and biology. She had begun to focus on how living things are affected by their environment. She wanted to know how **species** adapt to changes over time.

Francis Collins, director of the Human Genome Project, announces that a map of the human genome has been completed in April 2003. The project involved scientists from six countries and took thirteen years.

To find out, Kelley decided to study genomics. This field had sparked her curiosity. Even better, it used both math and science. She liked that she could combine her two main interests.

Kelley's next step was to go to graduate school at the University of Washington in Seattle. There she earned a PhD in genome sciences in 2008. She spent the next five years doing research in genomics. She worked at the University of Chicago and then at Stanford University. Her goal was to understand how humans have evolved over many thousands of years. How did our species adapt to big changes, such as where they lived or what they ate? Kelley wanted to use her understanding of genomics to find some answers.

## TECH TALK

"I majored in math in college, and as I was finishing up my degree I started thinking about my career. I realized I was so excited about math because it could be used to describe natural phenomena . . . [such as] patterns in leaves, so I added a biology major later on."

—Joanna L. Kelley

Kelley earned her doctorate in genome sciences from the University of Washington, which is located in Seattle.

## THE EVOLUTION OF GENES

Over millions of years, our planet has undergone many changes. These changes affect everything from the climate to the landscape. Life on Earth must adapt to survive those changes. But organisms don't adapt all at once. Changes to a species' body and brain happen very slowly. These changes are passed down from one **generation** to the next in a species' genes. This kind of change is known as **evolution**.

Kelley hoped to study evolution up close. She wanted to understand how individual genes adapt over time. One of her early projects involved researching a human gene called *enamelin*. This gene carries the instructions for making tooth enamel. Enamel is a hard, white material that helps protect our teeth from cavities. Kelley's work showed that *enamelin* had likely changed over time. But why? She argued that the gene adapted to a change in what early humans ate. Humans gradually switched from eating mostly leaves to eating harder foods. Chewing became harder work for teeth. *Enamelin* became thicker. It protected teeth from wear and tear.

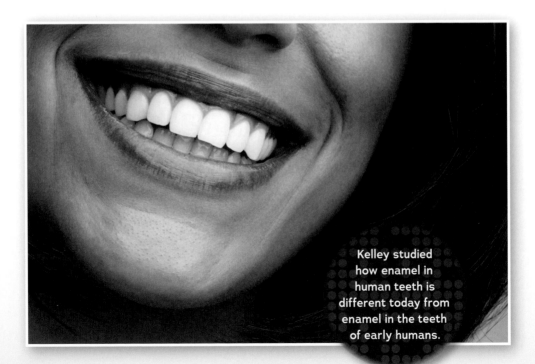

Kelley studied how enamel in human teeth is different today from enamel in the teeth of early humans.

## THE STUDY OF EVOLUTION

An Englishman named Charles Darwin made the idea of evolution famous. In the 1830s, he traveled the world studying plants, animals, and fossils. Darwin noticed that species change over time. He worked to understand why. In 1859, he published a book called *On the Origin of Species*. In it, he described evolution. His work later inspired many scientists, including Kelley.

Kelley's research was like one piece of a giant puzzle. It helped scientists better understand the story of human evolution. That story is full of many mysteries. Kelley hoped to help solve some of them.

## Chapter 3

Kelley spent time doing research on fish at McMurdo Station in Antarctica.

# GOING TO
# EXTREMES

Kelley's research soon branched out in new directions. She began to study other animals, not just humans. She was especially curious about animals that live in extreme environments. How do these species thrive in such harsh places? How do their genes adapt to help them survive? Kelley knew answers to those questions could be very valuable. Her

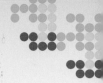

work could help scientists understand the evolution of other animals, including humans.

## FASCINATING FISH

To learn more, Kelley went to extreme environments. In Antarctica, she worked at a US research center called McMurdo Station. She studied the few kinds of fish that can survive in Antarctica's icy waters. Most fish will freeze to death in such a cold environment. But Kelley learned that Antarctic fish make substances called antifreeze proteins. These proteins prevent liquid from freezing in low temperatures. They protect the bodies of Antarctic fish. Kelley plans to unlock more secrets of these amazing creatures. It may take years of research to get all the answers. But Kelley doesn't mind.

This naked dragonfish makes an antifreeze protein that keeps it from freezing in the icy Antarctic water.

Kelley traveled to Mexico in May 2013 to study Atlantic molly populations. She and her team caught these fish from several different areas to collect samples of their genes.

Another focus of Kelley's research is a fish in Mexico called the Atlantic molly. Many Atlantic mollies live in streams full of a natural chemical called hydrogen sulfide. The chemical flows into the streams from nearby volcanoes. For most fish, the chemical is deadly. But the Atlantic molly has adapted to survive. Kelley wants to know how that happened. That's why she began studying the genomics of this unusual fish.

Kelley compares separate **populations** of Atlantic mollies to see how they have evolved over time. Not all Atlantic mollies live in streams that contain hydrogen sulfide. Those that do are genetically different from those that don't. They're also genetically different from ancient Atlantic mollies, which lived in less extreme environments. Studying these different populations tells Kelley how the species has adapted to different conditions over many generations.

One type of Atlantic molly is able to survive in chemical-filled streams.

# INTERESTING INSECTS

Kelley's curiosity didn't end with fish. She also studied a rare kind of insect called the Antarctic midge. This bug lives farther south than any other insect on Earth. It's also the largest land animal in Antarctica. Bigger Antarctic animals, such as penguins, spend at least some of their lives in the ocean. Only the midge spends its entire life on land.

This bug doesn't just survive extreme temperatures. It also gets by with very little water. That's because there's little to drink in Antarctica. Most of the continent's water is in the form of ice and snow. Yet somehow the Antarctic midge survives. Kelley is studying how this insect has adapted over time. Her research could someday change how scientists search for life on other planets with harsh environments.

The Antarctic midge is able to survive with little drinking water in the cold temperatures of Antarctica.

Studying the genomes of great apes, such as western gorillas, will tell scientists how certain species have adapted to changes in their environments.

## GREAT APES

Another group of animals, great apes, also caught Kelley's interest. Great apes include gorillas, orangutans, and chimpanzees. Their DNA is very similar to human DNA. That makes them especially interesting to study.

Kelley has helped to record the genomes of the great apes. This is one of her most urgent projects. Many great apes are in danger. Humans have taken over much of the land that apes once called home. This loss of land has made survival difficult for many apes. Some species of great apes are at risk of dying out. Kelley's work is helping scientists understand how great apes have adapted to change in the past. Her work could also help improve the chances of their survival in the future.

## HUMAN EVOLUTION

Kelley enjoys asking questions about fish, bugs, and apes. But she hasn't forgotten her first focus: humans. She has studied how early humans adapted to a major change in their environments.

Kelley and a team member keep track of genetic samples from Atlantic mollies in Mexico. Kelley studies these samples to learn how populations of this species have evolved.

## TECH TALK

"As a result of the genomics revolution scientists are acquiring a more complete picture of human evolution, the ways in which humans and other species adapt, and how diseases may ultimately be treated based on an individual's personal genome."

—*Joanna L. Kelley*

Most scientists believe that the human species evolved in Africa. Over time, some humans moved on foot to other parts of the world. In their new homes, they encountered different climates and new sources of food. Kelley has studied how and when human genes adapted to those changes. Her research will help scientists better understand the long history of human life on Earth.

Another kind of research Kelley is doing could help improve treatment for human diseases. Many diseases are passed down from parent to child through genes. Kelley's work can help doctors better understand the way our genes affect our health. That understanding could lead to better treatments.

## Chapter 4

Kelley *(third from left)* received a L'Oreal Women in Science Fellowship in 2012.

# AN ONGOING
# MISSION

Kelley's research has received attention from many other genome scientists. In 2012, she received a Women in Science Fellowship. The makeup company L'Oréal gives the award to young women who are doing important work in the sciences. The award provides up to $60,000 for scientific research. Kelley used the money for her research in genomics.

## PROFESSOR KELLEY

A big change happened for Kelly in 2013. That year, Washington State University in Pullman, Washington, hired her as an assistant professor. At the university, Professor Kelley set up her own laboratory for research. She called it the Kelley Lab.

Kelley began teaching at Washington State University in 2013.

At a 2013 conference, Kelley gave a presentation about the way technology helps genetic research.

Running the lab is a lot like running her own business. Kelley hires and trains students and scientists to work in the lab. She also raises money to keep the lab going. That way, she can continue learning about how life on Earth adapts to change.

Kelley's work at Washington State led to another great honor. In 2013, she was named one of twenty top young "investigators" working in genomics. The honor is given each year by *GenomeWeb*. This online publication shares the latest news about the field of genomics.

## INSPIRING OTHERS

The science of genomics inspired Kelley back when she was a college student. These days, Kelley is an inspiration to other young scientists. She shares her excitement and knowledge with the college students who work in her lab. She also inspires younger students, especially girls. She wants to encourage more girls and women to study math and science. That's why she became a mentor to girls through the Girl Scouts. She also helped start an organization called Women in Genome Sciences. This group of scientists works to make the field of genomics welcoming to women and minorities.

Kelley has inspired many Girl Scouts to pursue math and science careers.

Kelley's work as a mentor and a scientist continues to make a difference. She is always asking challenging questions. And she uses math and science to seek answers. Who knows where her curiosity will take her next?

## TECH TALK

"We need to have both men and women in all types of STEM [science, technology, engineering, and math] positions, at all levels, including high school science teachers, academic and faculty positions, as well as positions in professions in STEM companies and corporations. A greater breadth of experience needs to be open to everyone based on skill, not gender."

—*Joanna L. Kelley*

# TIMELINE

**1981**

Joanna L. Kelley is born.

**1996**

Scientists announce that they have discovered the complete genome for yeast.

**1999**

Kelley begins college classes at Brown University.

**2003**

The Human Genome Project announces a complete map of human DNA. Kelley graduates with a bachelor's degree in math and biology from Brown University.

**2008**

Kelley earns a PhD in genome sciences from the University of Washington. She goes on to do research at the University of Chicago.

**2010**

Kelley begins doing research at Stanford University.

**2012**

Kelley receives the Women in Science Fellowship for her research.

**2013**

Kelley becomes an assistant professor at Washington State University and opens the Kelley Lab. *GenomeWeb* names Kelley one of twenty top young investigators in the field of genomics.

# SOURCE NOTES

6  Susannah Meyer, "STEMinism: A Perspective from Women in STEM," For Girls in Science, May 28, 2013, http://forgirlsinscience.org/steminism-a -perspective-from-women-in-stem.

12  Ibid.

23  Joanna Lynne Kelley, "The Genomics Revolution," *Huffington Post*, November 19, 2012, http://www.huffingtonpost.com/joanna-lynne-kelley /genomics_b_2161232.html.

28  Meyer, "STEMinism."

# GLOSSARY

**biologist**
a scientist who studies life

**DNA**
the code that determines how an organism looks and functions

**evolution**
the way a life-form develops and changes over thousands or millions of years

**generation**
a group of living things born around the same time

**genes**
sections of DNA that control an organism's traits

**genome**
all the genetic material of a living thing, including its DNA

**genomics**
the study of genes and DNA

**organism**
a living thing

**populations**
members of the same species living in the same location

**species**
a particular type of living thing, such as a human

**traits**
characteristics that make one organism different from another and that are passed down through genes

# FURTHER INFORMATION

## BOOKS

Higgins, Nadia. *Life Science through Infographics*. Minneapolis: Lerner Publications, 2014. Learn more about the world of biology, including evolution and DNA.

Johnson, Rebecca L. *Amazing DNA*. Minneapolis: Millbrook Press, 2008. Dive into the exciting world of DNA.

Loxton, Daniel. *Evolution*. Toronto: Kids Can Press, 2010. Explore the amazing story of evolution on Earth.

## WEBSITES

**Joanna Lynne Kelley**
**http://forgirlsinscience.org/women-in-stem/joanna-lynne-kelley**
Check out this web page to learn more about Kelley and what inspired her to be a scientist.

**Meet our 2012 L'Oréal USA for Women in Science Fellow, Dr. Joanna Kelley!**
**https://www.youtube.com/watch?v=DKhCmbcnAC0**
Watch this short video to learn a little about Kelley and her Women in Science award.

**STEMinism: A Perspective from Women in STEM**
**http://forgirlsinscience.org/steminism-a-perspective-from -women-in-stem**
Learn about Kelley in her own words by reading this interview.

# INDEX

## ABOUT THE AUTHOR

Laura Hamilton Waxman has written many nonfiction books for young readers. She particularly enjoys writing about people such as Joanna L. Kelley who have shaped our world.